SCRIPTED SPONTANEITY!

Personal Scripts for Classic Magic

Jacques Lord

WRITE AWAY
BOOKS
Taking Authors From Idea to
Manuscript to Marketplace ™

TABLE OF CONTENTS

INTRODUCTION

Picture a hushed audience eyes locked on a performer who is defying physics, creating a new reality, blowing minds, and being the hit of the party at the same time! Don't look now, but that awe-inspiring performer is YOU!

"Easy to do!" "No practice necessary!" "Astonish your friends!" Well, that is what all those come-ons about learning magic tell us. Except the only thing the come-ons will successfully deliver is to separate you from your hard-earned money! Because if you don't believe you need practice and develop a minimal skill for writing your own patter, well your friends will be astonished all right. Astonished that you actually believed that carney barker tripe!

Though I am a part-time magician I still practice every day and rehearse on a regular basis. I write technical content and prose for a living as a full-time geologist. 10 to 12 times a year I perform professionally for a fee, and I always have a coin and a bandana in my pocket. I love magic and I have been working at my craft for over 50 years.

I am also a magician member of the Magic Castle in Hollywood since 2006, performing there in the member spaces every time I am there. In addition to the accolades from crowds of laypeople, I've got four First Place WINS at the local club level. Proud? Sure. And it helps to have top Professionals like Dennis Forel, Tom Frank, Joe Monte, Mike Stillwell, David Stryker, Phil Van Tee, and Kevin Viner critiquing and encouraging my personal scripting efforts. Thanks guys!

But note this: I am not at the level of a paid Castle performer… yet. But I do love magic and performing it for my audience - and the Castle staff always give me great feedback. Maybe you have never heard of me, but I still have something to offer you.

So, I want to give YOU my original efforts at scripting for several classic magic routines, and one effect I made up from scratch! I hope it inspires you to have the conviction of your own stories and insights, rather than memorizing the patter out of the box.

My thanks to all my magic mentors and colleagues, to my first teacher Biff Smith, to my daughters for putting up with a magician Daddy, and to my editors and publishers at Write Away Books! Rob Weinberg and his team are to writing and publishing as Dai Vernon is to Magic.

Please note: I have formatted my content so that spoken patter is in blue font.

Jacques P. Lord
West Sacramento, CA
April 1, 2026

COIN FROM THE EAR

It was the Holiday season a few decades back, and I had been hired to entertain a holiday party of disabled adults who were living in their own apartments with 24/7 professional caregivers. It was one of my first gigs as a professional. These were adults of all ages; 18 to 80, and they had a range of conditions, e.g., Cerebral Palsy, MS, Parkinsons. I came prepared to do my "best," my most sophisticated sleight of hand, for them. Boy, would I impress them! <sigh>

I was performing Dai Vernon's Cutting the Aces for a lovely young lady confined to a wheelchair, and I just knew she would react with wonder and amazement. Everyone did! But instead…

…she leaned over to me, stopped me in the middle of the card trick by putting her hands on mine and haltingly stated, "I don't get it." She looked at me with confusion and the bewilderment that was not the sort of reaction I was looking to create. Dai Vernon's words were ringing in my head; "Confusion is not magic."

[awkward pause]

Then she asked me, "Can you pull a coin from my ear?" She looked into my eyes with real interest; she wanted me to amaze her. I did as she asked, and her delight was palpable and gratifying. And that is when I decided that for my audience (handicapped or not), keeping it simple and giving my audience the wonder and laughter they wanted (and not pleasing my ego) was the best lesson.

Method

Pull out your favorite type of coin to manipulate – the bigger the better. I use a silver dollar.

"What is your first recollection of experiencing a magic effect? Was it your Granddad or Auntie pulling a coin from behind your ear? Everyone needs to know how to do it. And there are at least four methods!"

VARIATION 1: "We will start with the simplest. I take the coin in this hand (I use the finger palm almost like a French Drop, Photos 1 & 2. Note the open gap between fingers and coin grip in Photo 1 versus closed finger gap in Photo 2), and you blow on it (let the spectator blow; encourage them to really BLOW!)…and it VANISHES! And now I pull it from your ear! (make the suitable gestures)"

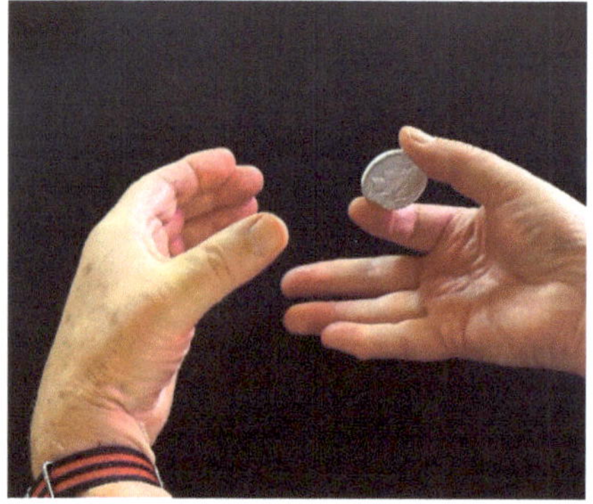
Photo 1

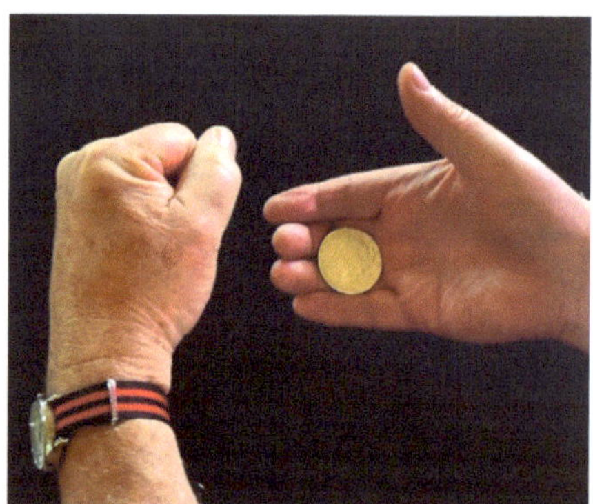
Photo 2

VARIATION 2: "The next more complicated level is to have me pass the coin from my hand to my other hand, and then I blow and it vanishes! Then I pull the coin from my…pocket!" Do a slightly more complex false transfer – e.g., classic palm. Blow on your own hand and show the coin has vanished. Pull the coin from your "back pocket." People usually laugh as if you pulled it out of your rear. If they do, look taken aback and ask them, "What are YOU thinking?" or "What's so funny?"

VARIATION 3: "Even more complicated is taking the coin at my fingertips, and again it is gone! But it is behind this ear over here!"

Do a fingertip to edge palm in your left as you false transfer to the right hand. Show both hands empty (watch the angles) for the first time and then pull the coin from the nearest ear. (Photos 3 & 4).

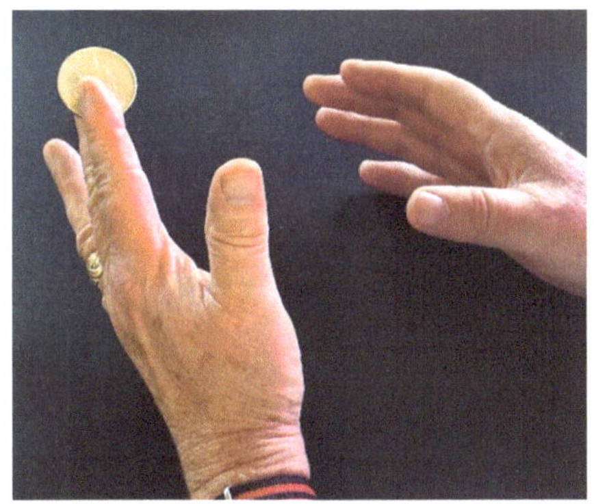

Photo 3

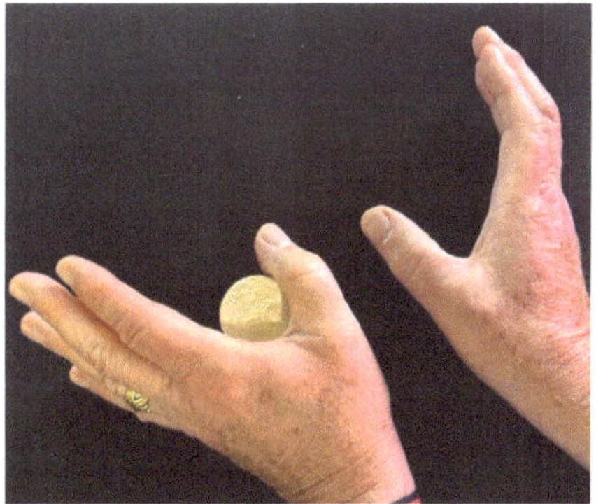

Photo 4

VARIATION 4: "The most difficult method of Coin behind the Ear has nothing to do with ears. You place the coin in your hand and rub the back of that hand and POOF! the coin is gone. But it is hidden on my thumb, and I can get the coin to reappear at my fingertips just like this…My other fingertips!"

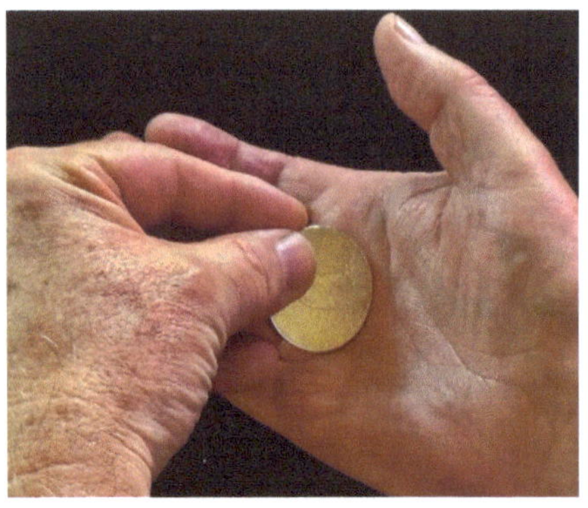

Photo 5

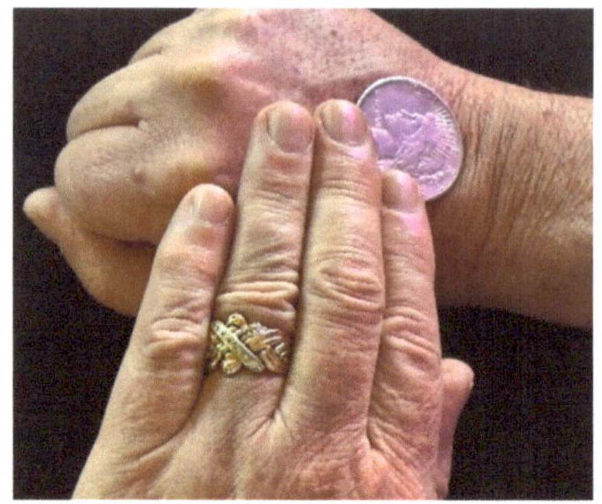

Photo 6

Falsely place the coin in your right hand with a retention vanish (Photo 5) and then place the coin on the back of right hand smoothly and quickly (Photo 6). Show each hand empty; slowly, one finger at a time. Watch the angles! (Photo 7) As you pull the coin "from my thumb" (left thumb) you let the coin drop from the back of your rotating right hand into your left hand as you "pull" the invisible coin off of your left thumb (Photo 8). Slowly rub the right fingers together until it is clear they are empty and point to the left hand (well out of the right-hand frame of reference) where the coin is displayed.

Photo 7

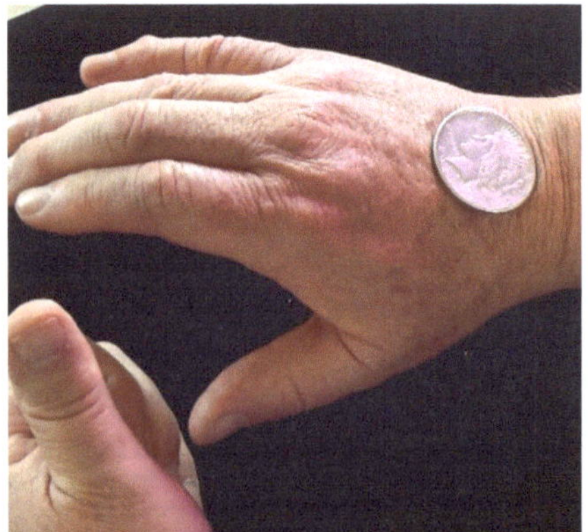

Photo 8

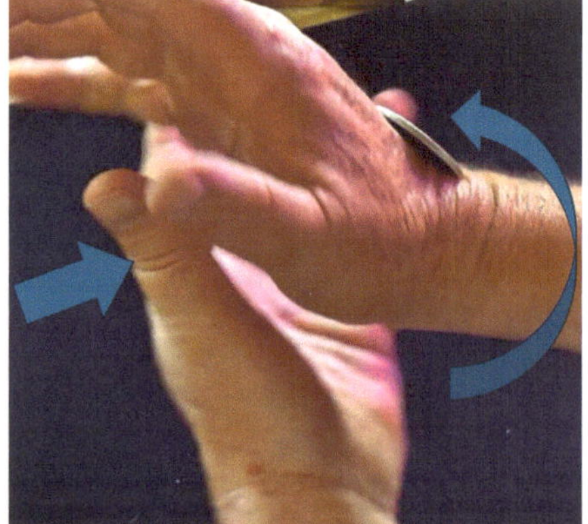

Grab the left thumb while rotating right hand and coin goes into left palm

PROF. BUNKMINSTER FULLOVIT

TEACHES ME MAGIC

A Chop Cup Routine

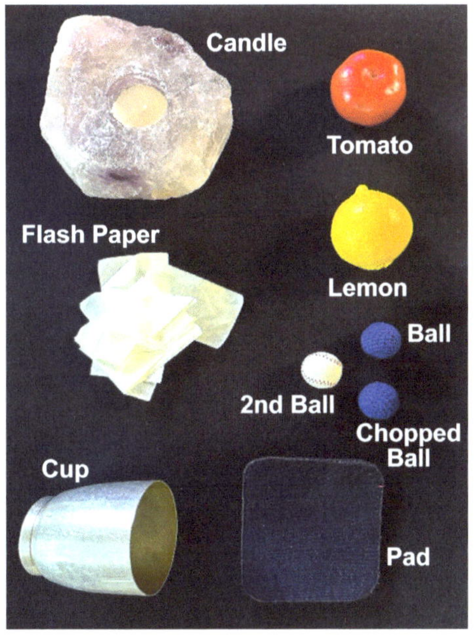

Photo 9

Photo 9. The candle in a holder (mine is a big chunk of amethyst) is lit, cup and post it-sized flash papers are on the table, and a regular ball is in finger palm in the right hand. The chopped ball and a bigger different-colored ball, a plastic lemon, and a plastic tomato are in my right pocket. The pad is only if needed to muffle the dislodging move.

"When I made the decision to pursue magic, I tried to find a rigorous academic program. And I found one at MIT, you know - the Milpitas Institute of Technology (or the La Jolla Institute of Irreproducible Results or your own made-up campus) and I took classes with Professor Bunkminster Fullovit."

Display the cup and flash papers. Wad up a flash paper in the left hand.

Touch the flash paper to the candle and toss the flame up. With the right hand, you -pluck- the palmed ball out of the flame.

 Light a second wad of flash paper and as you toss it up wave the flames loosely towards your mouth and feign inhaling the heat.

Place the ball in the cup and spill it out onto the table or into your hand a few times. Without saying so, you are demonstrating there is no magnet involved.

 Place the normal ball in the cup and then roll it into your hand and place the ball in your right pocket. Pick up the chopped ball in your pocket and finger palm the normal one. Display the chopped ball and place it into the cup. Pretend to place the chopped ball back into your right hand and display the normal ball. Place it in your right pocket while setting the cup down hard enough to dislodge the chopped ball.

 Lift the cup displaying the chopped ball.

The audience guesses and either way you can lift the cup exposing he chopped ball and respond, "You've seen this before!" (or) "You haven't got the hang of this yet but you will."

As you lift the cup exposing the chopped ball, go to your pocket and grab the 2nd larger ball and load it into the cup. Take the chopped ball with the left hand and place the loaded cup down with the right hand.

"How does this happen? I know you are smart people and if you think about it, you will recognize that I must be using two balls. (If the audience laughs use that misdirection to palm the lemon in your pocket.) And I do use two balls!" (Reveal the 2nd ball under the cup. As the second ball is released, kick it out a few inches with the cup edge and place the cup in the right hand, loading the lemon. Place the loaded cup on the table with the right hand as the left hand picks up the 2nd ball and place the 2nd ball on top of the loaded cup.

"So, I performed this for Prof. Fullovit and he graded me. And my grade was not what I expected. I got a lemon! And that is a very bad grade in the magician world." (While pattering palm the tomato from your pocket to your right hand ready to load the cup one last time. As soon as you reveal the lemon by lifting the cup with your left hand and kicking the lemon a few inches, transfer the cup to your right hand and load the tomato as you take the lemon in your left hand and display it. Using your right pinkie to keep the tomato in place, hold the loaded cup and gesture to the tomato and other balls on the table. Eventually place the cup down as you say

 (Lift the cup and reveal the tomato. Finish your routine by placing all the balls and loads back into the cup to demonstrate they can't all fit. Close with

NANOTECHNOLOGY

(Roy Walton's Card Warp)

I realize this script is very personal to my life and experience and not fit your personality or experience. But I am certain you can invent or derive your own intro to the Nanotechnology thread and go from there. The Isotope jokes are old, and I learned them from health physicists at the Oak Ridge National Weapons Lab when I was doing remediation and decontamination of the waste areas there in the early nineties.

"When I was a graduate Student at Rice University back in the 1980s, I read an article in the student newspaper about Rice Professor Richard Smalley's Nobel Prize-winning research into Nanotechnology. Nanotechnology is, as you well know, molecular-sized pumps and motors and gears and levers and such! Professor Smalley also discovered a carbon molecule of 60 carbon atoms bonded together in the shape of a soccer ball or geodesic sphere and named Buckminsterfullerene, more commonly known as Buckyballs. (If any of your audience indicates awareness of Dr. Smalley, you will have them in your hands like putty…)

Prof. Smalley had open office hours, so I made an appointment. He looked up at me as I came into his office and asked, "Who are you?" I replied I was a geology graduate student from across the quad, and I read the article about his nanotechnology research and,

I added as if it was obvious, I am a real fan of card tricks, and I was hoping you could help me apply nanotechnology to card magic?"

"Dr. Smalley looked at me like I had a Buckyball-shaped head and shrugging his shoulders as if he was thinking "Should I call Security or just make something up and hope he goes away." And then he spent 20 minutes of his incredible time and mind with me, and this is what we came up with." (Display the two cards previously prepared to perform Roy Walton's Card Warp. Photo 11) From this point on, the mechanics are as Roy Walton describes them. You can also add Paul Green's excellent augmented handling.)

Photo 11

"I take the two previously folded cards, and I fold the King lengthwise in half - face in. The two is folded widthwise face out. The spot card is now placed inside the face card which is folded face in. I invert the folded cards, and the King is now face out inside the two, folded face in. This is known mathematically as "orthogonal" or at 90 degrees and in opposite directions.

But this is not just two folded cards. Dr. Smalley and I figured out how to apply an isotopic reactor using the element Ignoranium to turn the folded cards into a time machine. The king is face out in the present, but as I move the king through the time tunnel... Observe. The molecular lattice of the king is inverted in the future and now both cards face in the same direction!"

(When passing the king through the tunnel, cover it with your hand and make a whistling/humming noise like a cheesy ray gun noise in a 60s Sci-Fi film. You whistle in a warble and hum simultaneously.)

"Unfortunately, the Ignoranium reaction is giving off atomic particles called BO-zons and MO-rons, so you are being exposed to radioactivity while the cards are in the future. Let's reverse the reaction and come back to the present time which will halt the radioactive decay. As a side note, Ignoranium decays to Administratium, which does not decay but reorganizes spontaneously every four years."

(Push the king through the tunnel back to the starting position, again covering it with your hand and make your whistling/ humming noise.)

"I know what you are thinking. This is a hokey card trick by some bloviating canard who is educated beyond his intelligence, but I am telling you NOOOOO! **This is real science!** (Insert exaggerated facial expressions of conspiratorial WE BOTH KNOW I AM BLOWING SMOKE here). I do not need to hide the cards with my hand nor make the whistling noise, although I do believe that enhances your experience. I only need to shove the card from the present to the future and let the nanotechnology do the rest. Once again you are being exposed to BO-zons and MO-rons and because I have your safety foremost in my mind, I will tear the cards and break the reaction and eliminate radiation, ensuring your safety."

(Tear the cards down the middle, destroying the evidence. Drop the pieces in someone's palm or the table surface. Photo 12)

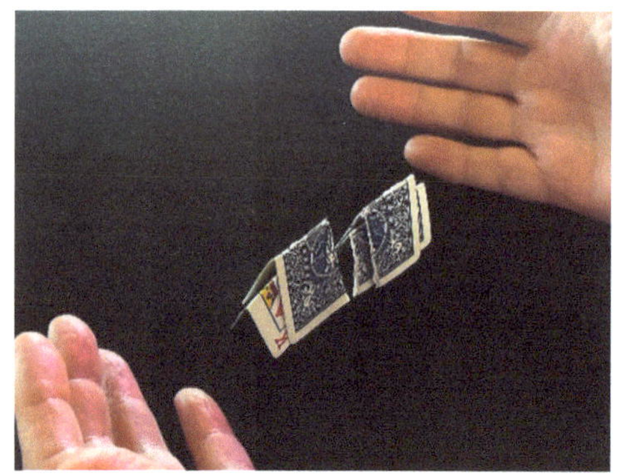

Photo 12

"And this is all there is.

And I have proven something scientifically beyond any doubt – irrefutable evidence that I do not play with a full deck."

CUPS N BALLS; MY FINAL LOADS

My Cups and Balls routine is Dai Vernon's routine straight out of **Stars of Magic (1975)** published by Tannen of New York. My only contribution is the final load sequence being two sets of three objects rather than the typical one. I use three polished stone spheres for the first final sequence that are in my right pocket, and the second final sequence is a limestone snail fossil and two plastic dinosaurs in my left pocket. Sometimes I use a handkerchief to keep the stone spheres from 'talking' in my pocket. More details on those load objects in a bit.

The spheres are approximately 2 inches in diameter. I use Sodalite (blue and white), Amethyst (purple) and Marble (black & white) because of their hardness and the color contrasts. As I reveal each ball, I name the mineral/rock and kick it out a bit to cover the loading of the cup for the second (and final) loads.

I challenge the audience after the reveal of the three spheres about being "Igneous, Metamorphic, and Sedimentary – WHAT'S MISSING?" I expect an answer, and usually some audience members step up to the challenge.

This sets up the second final sequence. The audience is wracking their brains trying to remember 4th grade earth science, but my question is a trick question. There is no fourth type of rock. Only three. But I explain I lift the middle cup revealing the snail shell.

And someone will shout out "Dinosaurs!" This perfectly cues up my lifting the last two cups on either side of the snail shell, revealing the two plastic dinosaurs, as I proclaim

Then I proceed to play 'puppets' with the two dinosaurs pretending that they are discussing the snail fossil. I hold them by their tails so the audience can see me playing with them like "action figures" or dolls, using my best cartoon voices to create the conversation between the toys like animated objects.

Use your best cartoon voices (I use a French accent to emphasize the escargot theme) and speak slowly so the audience can follow your silliness. Don't rush it.

I conclude with "That is enough silliness for one night! Thank you for playing along!"

I have lined my cups with black felt to reduce the 'talking' as I load the cups, but the felt is not foolproof. You must learn to load and place the loaded cup down quietly and it takes a lot of practice. The dinosaurs are quiet, but there is a knack to loading them and not having the tails stick out.

Here are my props for this routine (Photo 13):

Photo 13

The cups are lined with black felt. The snail shell is limestone and a tad soft making it appear somewhat beaten up but this does not detract from the effect. I collected my snail shell from the Glen Rose Formation outside of Austin, Texas.

The plastic dinosaurs came in a bag of dozens from an online vendor and I picked the ones with short arms and long tails for playing with them as puppets.

The 2-inch diameter polished spheres need to be hard so no fluorite or calcite or malachite or onyx or 'soapstone.' Rock shops and online sellers will have a wide selection, so you can choose based on color contrast and hardness (6.0 or more on the Mohs hardness scale). I suggest:

- Crystal quartz (clear)
- Amethyst (purple)
- Sodalite or lapis (blue)
- Marble (many colors)
- Zoisite corundum (green with red and black flecks)
- Petrified wood (multicolored quartz).

SewygE

(Smoke 'em while you got 'em)

This is a hand-made cigarette gag box set I make from wood. I sell them separately but here are my "instructions" to remove any doubts that, at almost 70 years old, I am still an immature doofus… "SewygE" can be pronounced SEW-edge, or seh-WEE-jee. This trick is about providing malevolent yet harmless disregard for social norms… Here's the thing: We all know smoking is lethal, toxic, rude, and socially unacceptable, so why not tweak and shock people's delicate sensibilities a little bit? Why not smoke (or try to light up) right in the most inappropriate places? Restaurants, medical building exam rooms, the office lunch/break room, or in an airport or bus? Everything is fair game with SewygEs.

Suggested Presentations

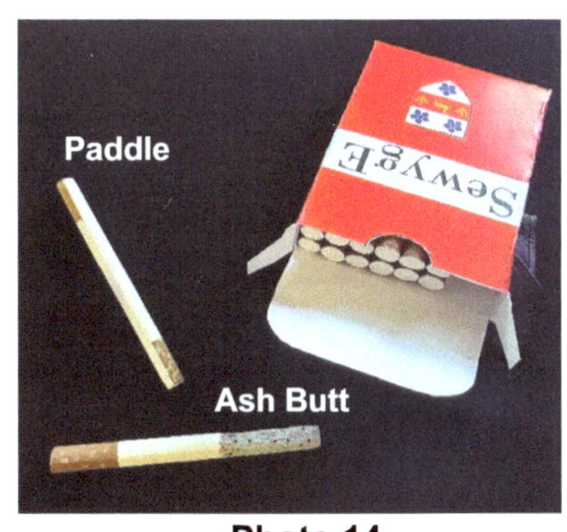

Photo 14

Performing with SewygE props (Photo 14) can be mostly done in mime or near silence. Try pulling the paddle out of the cigarette box provided and attempt to place it in your lips to light, but the cigarette refuses to cooperate – the tobacco end keeps ending up in your lips, much to your distaste! This can happen as you try to introduce yourself, but the cigarette interrupts you. Finally in frustration you mutter, "damn things are going to kill me anyway" and make it vanish. I used this presentation in one of my winning Ring 76 IBM parlor magic competition wins opening the act pretending to be Rod Serling introducing **The Twilight Zone** with the famous theme music on my phone.

You can be "smoking" the long ash prop as you approach diners at the restaurant table and gesture over their food or ask someone to hold out their hand as if it is an ashtray, you are about to use. Gesture over the buffet table or other food displays. Farmers' Market stalls could work.

Or sit in the Dr's exam room on your next appointment and surprise them with your unrepentant renewed smoking habit. Once you get a reaction, apologize and vanish the prop.

I drill 1/2" into the end of the ash butt out so I can load it with Baby Powder and flick the cigarette as I hold it, giving some semblance of "smoke."

THE SNEAKY SISTERS

Based on Bill Malone's version of Sam the Bell Hop

This effect is very old, and Bill Malone made it AMAZING! But the story is not "safe for work", if not downright misogynistic. I overheard Jeff McBride at the Castle tell a friend "You know, if someone could write an original script for Sam the Bellhop, that would be something."

So, I did. And if you are not familiar with the Herb Zarrow Shuffle? Learn it!

Here is the deck set up, top to bottom, for my version:

QC, QD, QS, QH, KH, AH, JC, JD, JS, JH, 6D, 5D, 4H, 2D, AC, KS, 6H, 5S, 4S, 2S, AD, KD, Blank card with the words "WHAT ARE YOU GIRLS DOING HERE?" written with a SHARPIE, 4D, 10C, 10D, 10S, 10H, 6S, 5H, 4S, Joker, Joker, Joker, 8S, 8D, 8H, 2H, 2C, 9D, 9S, 9H, 7H, 7S, 3C, 3D, 3S, 3H, AS, 9C, 8C, 7C, 6C, 5C.

PATTER:	METHOD:
This is the story of four sisters and their father as told with a shuffled deck of cards. They live with their father, and he is trying his best to raise them.	Zarrow Shuffles False Cuts: repeat as you talk and do not look at your hands.
Now believe you me, if you are a parent of teenage daughters, this is one of the scariest scenarios imaginable. I have four daughters myself but any resemblance of the four sisters in this story to my own girls is STRICTLY coincidental! So let me introduce you to the sneaky sisters, Julia, Heather, Celeste, and Phoebe. The fact that their names are the same as my daughters is again - coincidental.	Produce the four queens in order Q1, Q2, Q3 and Q4.
These girls were the apples (Ace of hearts) of their Father's eye (King Hearts). But being overprotective he tended to smother his girls as he knew what was out there in the real world.	Deal out AH KH Zarrow then hand the deck to spectator.

<table>
<tr><td>

</td><td>

Spectator cuts deck

</td></tr>
<tr><td>

</td><td>

Charliere cut, standard table cut, Charliere to get back to initial order. Deal out J – J – J – J

</td></tr>
<tr><td>

</td><td>

False cut into 3 piles and pick up and false cut to restore order

</td></tr>
<tr><td>

</td><td>

Deal out 6–5-4 <pause> 2–1

</td></tr>
<tr><td>

</td><td>

Deliver this line like it is a no brainer.

</td></tr>
<tr><td>

</td><td>

Deal a K, then
Zarrow Shuffle

</td></tr>
<tr><td>

</td><td>

Same spectator cuts deck. Charliere cut, standard table cut, Charliere to get back to initial order, Deal out 6-5-4…2-1

</td></tr>
</table>

Club, where he was sure he'd find them playing 21.	
He walks in, sees his girls, and do you know what he says?	Deal the K.
"Say STOP!" "OK, now read your chosen card in a stern dad voice!"	Riffle and slip cut force the **"What are you girls doing here?"** card to an audience member. This moment is REALLY fun for everyone.
Well, the four boys realized they'd gotten off on the wrong foot with Dad! So, all four went to him (Cut the cards please) and said "What we did was wrong. But your girls are old enough to be here and our intentions are honorable. Tell you what, we'll each fork over $10 so you can have a steak dinner here at the Club and be our chaperone!"	Zarrow Shuffle then false cut Deal the 4 Same spectator cuts deck. Charliere cut once to get back to initial order, Deal out 10 – 10 – 10 – 10
The father considered their plan and decided this would be a great teaching opportunity. "Boys" he said, "I used to come often to the 654 Club myself, but I didn't play 21, I played poker. Watch and learn as I take your $40	False cut (different than prior ones) Deal the K False overhand shuffle before dealing out the 6 – 5 – 4

and turn it into enough money to buy us ALL a steak dinner. Because you are right, I need to get to know you. Now, go find me some card players!"

So, the boys combed the club and found three jokers who thought they could play poker.

They anted up and the dad dealt four hands of 5-card stud, no draw. Money was on the table!

The first player had a full house, eights over twos! But he didn't win. The second player had a full house of nines over sevens! But he didn't win either.
Because the third player had four threes and an Ace high!
The three gamblers looked at the dad, and he knew the only way to win and buy all those dinners was to hold a small straight flush.

Which he had!

False overhand shuffle and pull each individual joker off singly before pulling packets to keep the deck order.

Deal Joker – Joker – Joker

False overhand and then deal each hand as the script indicates.

Stand as you deliver your closing line and accept the accolades you have earned.

GUMPER'S HARMONICA

("Gumper" was my dad. He loved harmonica playing and he was my inspiration for this bit of ambitious madness)

IMPORTANT: This is a stage or parlor effect – not suited for close-up.

Effect: Performer comes up to the mic or stage front and announces he would like to play his harmonica to warm the audience up like a campfire sing-along! (you can also insert Robert Klein's harmonica routine about using the harp as a healthcare monitor, but credit Mr. Klein).

Performer plays a quick scale or full draw/blow to warm up. He then asks all to sing along and just as he brings the harp to his lips, it crumples into a wad of paper. The performer is startled but tries to keep calm and brings out a second harp. He makes sure it is solid and plays a blow/draw to be sure. He once again asks all to sing along.

The Performer launches into Bach's _Jesu, Joy of Man's Desiring_. This piece has no words, and the audience is confused (some will get the joke). Performer slows down and stops playing as he realizes no one is singing along. "Oh, right! No words to that one. OK let's try this one!" Then performer launches into the _Flintstones Theme_, or the _Mexican Hat Dance_, or J. Geil's _Whammer Jammer_, any tune that is recognizable and **the performer can play well**. At the finish the audience applauds as the performer takes a bow. Performer sets harmonica back up to his mouth to play some more but is shocked to realize his harp has vanished again from his hands.

Frustrated, bewildered, close to panic, the performer goes to his procedures manual (The book **Magic for Dummies**) and looks up "Harmonica; what to do when it vanishes unexpectedly." The text instructs the performer to remember that music is nothing more than vibrating air molecules, so gather up some of the remnant vibrations hanging around from the last time you played, and form them into an invisible harmonica, which by definition cannot vanish as it is already invisible. IF the performer can do this, he will have regained control of the situation and can conclude his performance successfully.

"Plucking" remnant vibrations from the air the performer crams the molecules into his hand and blows a few notes of a scale. One note is missing and he plucks a few more molecules and completes his invisible harp. He proceeds to play a few bars of _"The Stars and Stripes Forever"_ and punctuates the tune with a cartoony coda like _"Shave and a haircut, two bits!"_

As he bows at this completion point, he doffs his hat and wipes his brow with a handkerchief, then pockets the bandana and replaces his hat on his head to show his hands are empty.

Alternate ending: No hat. The handkerchief can be used to mop your brow, then produce a REALLY BIG harmonica a la Johnny Ace Palmer producing a coke bottle, saying "If you didn't know what an invisible harp looks like, here's one!"

Method:

There are three or four magic moments to this routine.
    1. The first harp crumples into paper
    2. The second harp vanishes completely
    3. An invisible harp is created and played
    4. Optional - Invisible harp is revealed as a 6-inch monster harp

Figure 1

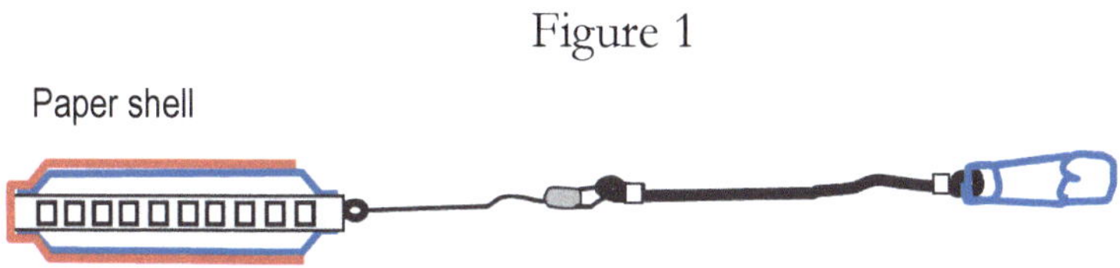

Figure 1 shows the set up for the first harp turning into paper. This simple pull is in the sleeve and hardwired with a small eyebolt to the harmonica with an eyebolt. The paper shell is standard white copy paper you wrap around the harp, and tape and trim to make a sleeve over the harp. Use Sharpies with black, silver, and gold coloration on your paper shell to mimic the harmonica (Photo 15). Blow into the holes when you introduce the act, then turn to the side that the sleeve is loaded and drop the harp to your side. Let it go up your sleeve with your body turned to hide any fabric movement. Then bring the shell up to your lips and crumple it like it has a life of its own.

The second vanish is accomplished by a pull designed by Bob Pozner. He called it the "bug" (See Figure 2 and Photo 16) and it has a neodymium magnet with a hook. Because a Hoener harp like a Blues harp or Marine Band or Special 20 is so heavy, it is necessary to place a thin neodymium under the metal harp cover (Figure 3). Now the bond between the bug and harp magnets is so strong, there is no risk of the harp being flung on to the floor.

Figure 2

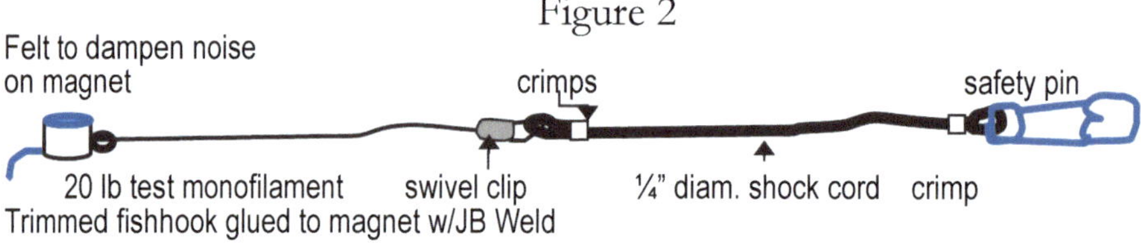

Figure 3

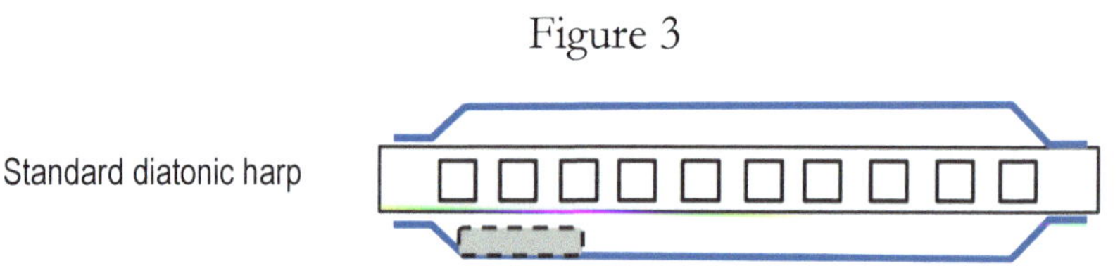

Niobium Magnet (the magnet affects the reeds it is close to, so work out the best location for this magnet iteratively. Location depends on which hand holds the bug as well.)

The bug is pinned to my jacket at the inner collar facing the nape of my neck. The bug is also stretched into my left trouser pocket and hooked into the material. I pull the harp out of my inner jacket pocket on the right side to have the harp in my left hand – the hand I hold it to play. I proceed to explain what I am about to do and handle the harp nonchalantly but obviously it is a free object to the audience without calling their attention to that fact. Once that is done, I steal the bug with my left hand from the left pocket, get the hook in the crook of my thumb, and attach it to the harp as silently as possible. Use patter to hide the thud as the felt on the bug magnet is good for 70%-80% noise dampening and you must misdirect to "dampen" the remaining sound.

The harp is now ready to vanish. Play your pieces of music. Bow at the conclusion of the piece in a dramatic, diva-worthy bow. You let the harp go at the bottom of the bow. This takes a LOT of practice in front of both a mirror and people. The harp is big and can catch on your jacket. You almost have to toss it with a flick to your body to avoid the jacket snag.

Your hands remain cradled around the harp as you bow, and they remain cradled around nothing as you stand back up straight. Bring the hands to your mouth as you announce you will play another short piece. **At this point the acting is critical.** You have to believe the harp just vanishes from your hands at that moment. Show your hands empty, dramatically. Be astonished! Be worried. [You are separating the method from the magic moment.] The act just went sideways, and you have no idea why or what to do about it.

With your harp gone, you search frantically through your pockets to find another, but you do not have one.

Actually, you do. It is a Hoener mini 4-hole harp (Photo 16). It has a lanyard loop, so you know which end is the lower note and which the higher.

With the mini harp stolen and palmed, you get out your manual, ***Magic for Dummies***, and read the section on how to recover a vanished harmonica. Speak *sotto voce* so the audience can follow your thought process and what the book is telling you to do. You are separating the method from the magic. **NOTE:** There is no real "Harmonica; what to do when it vanishes unexpectedly." section in the book *Magic for Dummies*. The sections above gives you the script you need to keep your "story" moving forward.

Begin snagging remnant vibrations of music out of the air. [Believe me it looks a lot better than the stupid dove net.] Once you think you have enough, play a scale on the mini harp but leave out one note (La or Ti). Grab a few more molecules and complete the scale. Now you can play The Stars and Stripes Forever or some other tune of your choosing, but the mini is difficult to play so keep it easy and quick. It will only take two measures to amaze the audience and two more measures to bore them.

Palm the mini and take another bow. Everyone is watching your hand. You take your hat off (if you wear one) and bow as you use your other hand to grab a handkerchief in your chest pocket and wipe your brow. With both hands holding something the audience is confused as to where the mini is. Replace the hanky and then use that free hand to place the hat on your head, with the mini harp ditched into the hat or pocket.

Adam Gussow, PhD, U of Mississippi is the best of many online harp teachers. His web video lessons on playing a harp are fantastic and worth the subscription fee. www.modernbluesharmonica.com.

I use regular bond paper, and Sharpies – a brown one, black one, and silver one – and Xacto knife out the holes in front and vent slits in back to get it to play.

Photo 15

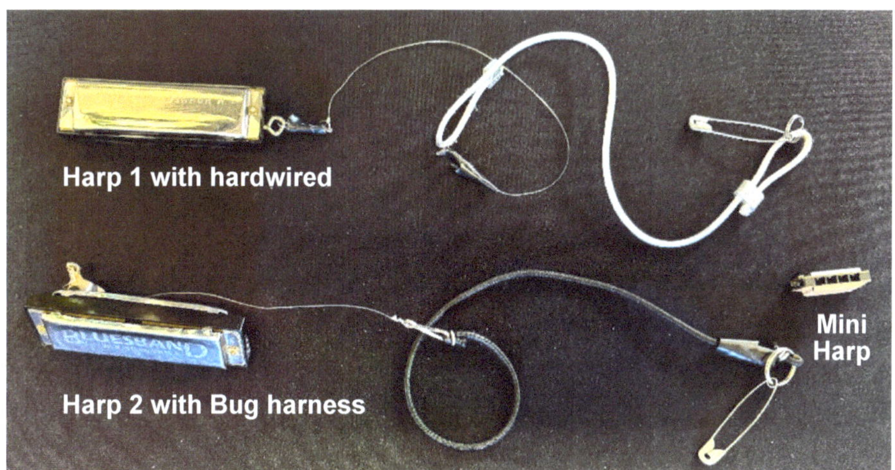

Photo 16

Conference Call Magician...

Well, that's it. I'm not a famous magician but I love magic and I want to contribute to the Art by example. I hope you got something out of my efforts. Best advice I ever got? Keep practicing and rehearsing and performing and WRITING!

And if you ever have any questions about this, or anything else, I will make up an answer. That's the consultant in me. So…maybe ask someone else…

jacquesplord@gmail.com